Pavilion Propositions

John Macarthur
Susan Holden
Ashley Paine
Wouter Davidts

Valiz

Pavilion Propositions

Nine Points on an Architectural Phenomenon

Studies in Art and Architecture

Contents

Like the pavilions that are its topic, this book is modest in scale and ambiguous in genre, while taking up the challenge to make concrete propositions. The contemporary pavilion, a seemingly pocketable topic, can be unpacked in so many directions that it threatens to encompass the whole of architectural culture. In fact, we began with a particular though difficult question that the pavilions seem to raise: is architecture art?[1] This is a question has been answered in the affirmative and in the negative at different times and places in cultural history. What interests us is not the answer, but rather the points at which this impossible question arises, what brings it back to the surface of discourse, and what is displaced through this process. The current pavilion phenomenon is one of those moments that are ripe for analysis. The book is not an argument for

7

1   This text has been prepared as the first significant piece of research undertaken by the ARC funded Discovery Project: *Is Architecture Art? A History of Categories, Concepts and Recent Practices*, which takes an expansive look at the exchanges between art and architecture in the present, and in the context of their histories. It was first presented as a discussion paper to open the conference, *Inside/Outside: Trading Between Art and Architecture*—the inaugural event of the project held in Ghent in Spring 2017. The conference was organised by the Centre for Architecture, Theory, History and Criticism (ATCH) at the School of Architecture, University of Queensland, in partnership with the Department of Architecture & Urban Planning, Ghent University, and in collaboration with the Royal Academy of Fine Arts (KASK), School of Arts, Ghent. Participants in the conference were Angelique Campens, Guy Châtel, Wouter Davidts, Mark Dorrian, Susan Holden, Maarten Liefooghe, Mark D. Linder, John Macarthur, Philip Metten, Ashley Paine, Emily E. Scott, Léa-Catherine Szacka, Annalise Varghese, Stefaan Vervoort, Stephen Walker, and Rosemary Willink. Respondents to the text at the conference were Lara Schrijver and Wouter Van Acker.

   Earlier versions of the text benefited from insightful comments from Catharina Gabrielsson, Jordan Kauffman, Maarten Liefooghe, Annalise Varghese and Rosemary Willink.

pavilions or pavilion programs. We are not pundits, and are indifferent as to whether more pavilions will, or should, be built. Similarly, nothing that follows constitutes advice or criteria for what makes a good, progressive, or even interesting pavilion, nor are there warnings against their corrupting effects. What concerns us is the phenomenon: the shifting cultural terrain that has caused a new commonplace to emerge.

Given our starting point, we have concentrated our attention on a particular kind of high-art pavilion: those non-permanent yet often flamboyant architectural appendages to visual arts institutions, designed in the main by high-profile architects. This focus may seem narrow, as it is common to observe that there has been a much wider proliferation of such pavilions and pavilion programs in recent times. They constitute a new aspect of contemporary culture that is extensively documented in professional publications and in the design blog sphere. Undoubtedly, the art pavilions that interest us are part of a wider phenomenon of temporary pop-up structures and the changing temporality of urban event-based culture.

Nevertheless, our specific interest in pavilions linked to art institutions has been triggered by the categorical blurring produced by many such commissions. The Serpentine Galleries' annual pavilion

8

program (since 2000) for London's Kensington
Gardens is widely considered the archetype, and, as
such, serves as a subject and key point of reference
for our research. The resulting spectacle-making
edifices operate between objects and buildings, or,
between buildings and sculptures, as they are both
on display and in use. At base, there is also a pro-
ductive ambiguity in the scale of the pavilion, which
allows one to apply a gallery view so as to see architecture as an artwork, or at least, as an art-like object.
The similarities in scale and commissioning of the
pavilions with much installation art are such that, at
times, it seems only their disciplinary categories separate them. This book aims to scrutinize this fundamental ambiguity concerning the status of the work,
in the issues of commissioning, curation, construction, value, and disciplinary determination.

The popular and wide-spread adoption of the
pavilion suggests that it is both amorphous and
inclusive: it remains open to appropriation and
resists strict categorization. This is why, in common
parlance, pavilions are only ever loosely defined:
as small or secondary structures (but not always);
mostly ornamental or ancillary in function (but are
sometimes fully fledged buildings); in appearance, or
in fact, described as seasonal, ephemeral or peripa-
tetic (but they are just as likely to be permanent); and
are frequently said to demonstrate an experimental,

9

frivolous or speculative aesthetic, associated with pleasures of exhibition and display, of seeing and being seen. Pavilions can be any of these things, and much else besides.

Although difficult to define, the concept of the 'pavilion' marks a well-known relation of architectural practice to a type of building commission and construction. As a mode of practice, they are a relatively accessible way for architects to engage in innovative commercial and civic forms, and in high culture. Similarly, in architecture schools, there is a history of andragogy where pavilions are set as exercises in imagination, and for formal and material exploration. We don't propose that our focus on the high-art end of this phenomenon can explain this wider spectrum of practice. The book offers some perspective on such tasks, but not directions.

Despite the ubiquity of pavilion construction today, and an enormous volume of words announcing, describing and judging them, little has been written on their place in the wider cultural landscape. In the rare moments of discourse on art and architecture where the pavilion phenomenon is considered as a cultural moment or nexus, the pavilions are treated as symptomatic of an exhaustion of the critical potential of architecture and the visual arts. Their 'arty-ness' is said to betray the social and technical ambitions of architectural avant-gardes past, or, their 'architectural-ness' is taken to be a Trojan horse for neoliberal values in art institutions. We propose that such a rush to judgment risks overlooking the new confluence of familiar and emerging concepts and categories in pavilion design and construction. We argue that the pavilion phenomenon has more to tell us about the changing position of architecture in culture and, in particular, its relation with: the concept of 'art' per se, the visual arts, the categorization of art disciplines, and something of the institutions themselves—from museums to cultural policy—that make and erode these categories.

This question of categorization and whether it has a conceptual basis or is merely a matter of professional boundaries is key for us. Not because we think that it can be properly resolved but, rather, because we aim to unravel the knot in which past concepts produce current categories that require critical reconceptualization. The pavilions are not just some epiphenomenon of the ongoing history of the idea of art and its 'departments.' Rather, they occasion a moment, or an event, in which new categories of practice are produced that shift our very concept of architecture.

A set of nine propositions organize the book. The first offers a rebuke of the adage that the pavilion is an over-used and obsolete subject for critical practice and discourse. Subsequent propositions address aspects of the pavilion's contemporary use and recent past: its critical reception in architecture and the visual arts, as well as its intersection with other fields that continue to condition any pavilion-like structure that is commissioned, designed and eventually built: history, discipline and economy. Together, the nine propositions are presented as a map of how the contemporary pavilion phenomenon opens up significant issues for the place of architecture in culture.

1

That the proliferation of pavilions is a symptom of changes in the cultural field that are affecting the concept of architecture.

With every new exhibition of a temporary, largely functionless, construction commissioned from an architect by a visual arts institution, there is a reverberation. Whatever the merits of the individual work, it is nearly impossible not to hear and then remark on the apparent ubiquity of 'pavilions, pop-ups and parasols.'[2] The emergence of the contemporary pavilion phenomenon is often attributed to the Serpentine Galleries' first pavilion in 2000 commissioned by then director, Julia Peyton-Jones. The immense popularity of these seasonal structures in the parkland setting of Kensington Gardens is believed to have shifted the broader cultural landscape within just a few short years. Certainly, by 2012—London's Olympic year—the Serpentine program had achieved significant public familiarity and cultural ubiquity. The design of that year's pavilion

2   Leon van Schaik and Fleur Watson, *Pavilions, Pop-ups and Parasols: The Impact of Real and Virtual Meeting on Physical Space* (London: John Wiley & Sons, 2015).

15

3 Sylvia Lavin, 'Vanishing Point,' *Artforum International* 51, no. 2 (October 2012).

4 MoMA PS1's YAP cemented itself as a program for young architects in 2000 to mark the affiliation of MoMA and PS1, after two previous projects staged at the venue, then known as PS1 Contemporary Art Center. The first in 1998 by the Vienna based artist group Gelatin (continuing the institution's long-standing practice of commissioning installation art); the second in 1999 by Philip Johnson (the first project by the newly merged institution). Both MoMA PS1's YAP and the Serpentine Galleries' pavilion program developed out of an emerging pattern of creating festive temporary structures for parties and events hosted by the institutions. See: The Museum of Modern Art, 'Young Architects Program (YAP),' http://momaps1.org/yap/.

5 The Australian programs include: The Sherman Contemporary Art Foundation's (SCAF) Fugitive Structures (2013–2016); the Naomi Milgrom Foundation's MPavilion (with support from City of Melbourne and the Victorian State Government) (2014–2019); and The National Gallery of Victoria's NGV Architecture Commission (2015–).

by Herzog & de Meuron and Ai Weiwei, based as it was on a cumulative archaeology of the footprints of all the past Serpentine Pavilions, led to claims that the format had become self-referential, and that the pavilion idea had been so relentlessly copied that there was nowhere left for it to go.[3]

Although it sits as an origin point and exemplar of the phenomenon, the Serpentine Galleries' pavilion program is not an isolated case. There are many programs and their strategies are varied. MoMA PS1's Young Architects Program (YAP, which is described as an 'installation') began almost simultaneously with the Serpentine program, and has now expanded from its concrete-walled courtyard in Queens, New York to include four additional international venues: CONSTRUCTO Santiago (since 2010); MAXXI Rome (since 2011); Istanbul Modern (biannually since 2013) and MMCA Seoul (since 2014).[4] The Serpentine Galleries too have experimented with the expansion of their pavilion program, spawning four additional 'Summer Houses' in 2016, as well as a design-your-own-pavilion competition for children, begun in 2015. Meanwhile, public and private institutions around the world have tried to emulate the success of the Serpentine and YAP examples. In Australia, for example, at least three separate programs have been instigated since 2013.[5] Today, pavilions are so widespread that online journal *ArchDaily* has at least four separate tags to capture this most diverse and elusive breed of architecture.[6] *The Architectural Review* even initiated a new Pop-up Award for the first time in 2016 to celebrate forms of temporary architecture that have been conventionalized by the pavilion phenomenon. And, as we write this essay, new programs continue to be announced, such as the Dulwich Pavilion, commissioned by the Dulwich Picture Gallery, which had its first instantiation in the summer of 2017.

All indications are that there has been a measurable increase in the number of pavilions, and a rapid expansion of popular and commercial interest in them as well.[7] It is also clear that, within the broader cultural context of pop-ups and temporary urban structures, pavilions have become a commonplace of practice: no longer the domain of the up-and-coming, or a stepping-stone to more substantial commissions, but a respectable mode of architectural production of the mainstream as well. These kinds of projects have even become the mainstay for some practices—such as LIKE architects, NEON, and Atelier YokYok—that combine experimental architecture, art and design for temporary constructions and stylish event spaces.

Invariably, one wonders whether we are witnessing a bubble that has inflated rapidly in a circum-

6   The 'Cultural Architecture' category collects projects under rubrics including 'Pavilion,' 'Installation' and 'Temporal Installations,' while the 'Landscape & Urbanism' category contains a further group titled 'Installations & Structures.' See: *ArchDaily*, www.archdaily.com/.

7   While it is difficult to quantify the scale of the pavilion phenomenon, there is some numerical data to evidence its growth. In our research we studied the number of projects documented on popular online design magazines during the years 2010 and 2015. For the year of 2010, forty-five pavilions were identified using the aggregated search results of three popular architecture websites. We used *Dezeen*, *ArchDaily* and *Metalocus*. The same search terms produced more than 170 results for 2015. Our method was hardly scientific, but the near four-fold increase observed is still remarkable. Correlated against trends in related internet search terms, a pattern of impressive growth is again perspicuous. For example, an analysis of the phrase 'Serpentine Pavilion' using Google Trends reveals mid-year peaks in user searches that align with each pavilion's summer unveiling, typically in early June each year. It also shows that the phrase has more than doubled in search popularity over the past decade, reaching an all-time peak in 2016. Google Trends explains that it measures changes in interest over time: 'Numbers represent search interest relative to the highest point on the chart for the given region and time. A value of 100 is the peak popularity for the term. A value of 50 means that the term is half as popular. Likewise, a score of 0 means the term was less than 1% as popular as the peak.' Google Inc., 'Google Trends,' https://trends.google.com.au/trends/.

8   Other examples include peak beard, peak internet kitten, and peak porn. 'Peak peak' was announced by *The Guardian* in 2014: Paula Cocozza, 'Have We Reached Peak Peak? The Rise (and Rise) of a Ubiquitous Phrase,' *The Guardian*, 28 August 2014, www.theguardian. com/media/2014/aug/27/ have-we-reached-peak-peak-rise-ubiquitous-phrase.

stance where growth cannot be unlimited. Have we indeed reached 'peak pavilion' as some critics claim? In recent years, the use of 'peak' as an adjective has moved from the serious matter of oil price and supply to become a common usage for cultural phenomena, which are held to be past their prime, in need of correction, and soon to fall into an inevitable decline.[8] While many perceive a direct correlation between the continued proliferation of pavilions and a loss in their criticality and cultural import, whether or not we have reached 'peak pavilion' may not be the right question to ask.

While we concur that the pavilion phenomenon has reached, and passed, a kind of threshold, we nonetheless question whether that threshold is one defined by a point at the top of a bell-shaped graph. Instead, we propose to interpret the ubiquity of pavilions as a means of rethinking notions of normativity and criticality. We seek to ask: what is at stake in considering the contemporary pavilion to have become a cultural norm? The emergence of a new commonplace is a rare and remarkable event in culture. Critics of the pavilion phenomenon treat it as a cliché that simplifies complex problems and stops thought. This might be true of particular pavilions, or programs, but we don't think it a useful characterization of the pavilion as a cultural phenomenon. We are more interested in the power or effectivity of

18

the pavilion as an idea and how, and in what conditions, it has emerged. Hence, we come down on the side of Baudelaire who once suggested that: 'Creating a cliché, now that's genius.'[9]

Seeing pavilions as symptoms of the decline of critical culture in architecture runs the risk of misunderstanding the issues at stake in their emergence: namely, their present-day role in the discipline and practice of architecture on the one hand, and the wider cultural shifts affecting the concept of architecture on the other. In our analysis we are interested in understanding the density of historical forces and cultural self-awareness that have forced them into existence as an unavoidable presence in contemporary art and architecture. To these ends, the following propositions draw on existing literature across fields of architecture, art and cultural policy, as well as our own analysis of the phenomenon, to make a comprehensive account of the issues in positioning the pavilion.

9 'Creating a cliché, now that's genius. I must create a cliché,' 'Mon coeur mis à nu,' no. 36, Charles Baudelaire *Oeuvres completes*, pp. 638. cf. Walter Benjamin and Harry Zohn, *Charles Baudelaire: A Lyric Poet in the Era of High Capitalism* (London: NLB, 1973); Graham Robb, 'The Poetics of the Commonplace in *Les Fleurs Du Mal*,' *The Modern Language Review* 86, no. 1 (1991), pp. 57–65.

2

That assessments of the pavilion phenomenon need to account for the relation of architecture and the visual arts.

10 Leon van Schaik, 'On Pavilions,' *Architecture Australia* 105, no. 2 (2016), 40.

Critical consideration of the broader issues that interest us is rare, particularly concerning the intersection of architecture and the visual arts. The majority of publications on the pavilion phenomenon provide only documentation and exegesis of particular examples, published in catalogues and the blog-sphere where the little critical writing that is included serves only to inflate the hype of recent pop-up culture with thinly veiled promotion of the latest designs. Even informed commentators are typically advocates for pavilions. Leon van Schaik, for instance, extolls the accepted belief that pavilions are 'uniquely suited to releasing and distilling speculations on new architectures.'[10] Likewise, Philip Jodidio, the preeminent exegete of the Serpentine program, writes of pavilions as opportunities for architectural experimentation:

The image they define of contemporary architecture is far more relevant and revealing than any selection of 'real' buildings might be, because those who design them can afford to play with the rules ... stretching the limits of architecture into new territories that will surely go on to have a significant impact on more 'solid' structures.[11]

Jodidio's blatant endorsement of the innovative and experimental nature of the present-day pavilion is typical of much of the discussion in the popular and professional press. It is, however, challenged by a few authors who have put the phenomenon to a more critical and historical examination, albeit without much agreement. Important historical overviews by the likes of Barry Bergdoll and Joel Robinson, for example, are skeptical of the aesthetic and formal novelty displayed by today's pavilions, undercutting the hype of commentators such as Jodidio.[12] At the same time, a number of other notable academics— namely Beatriz Colomina, Sylvia Lavin and Andrea Phillips—have tended to historicize, and measure, the current phenomenon primarily against the experimental and socially ambitious pavilions of progressive architects in the early and mid-twentieth century. Not surprisingly, in comparison to these emancipatory projects, most current pavilions are deemed disappointing: they have lost their critical

11 Philip Jodidio, *The New Pavilions* (New York: Thames & Hudson, 2016), p. 7.

12 Barry Bergdoll, 'The Pavilion and the Expanded Possibilities of Architecture,' in *The Pavilion: Pleasure and Polemics in Architecture*, ed. Peter Cachola Schmal (Ostfildern: Hatje Cantz, 2009); Joel Robinson, 'Introducing Pavilions: Big Worlds Under Little Tents,' *Open Arts Journal* 2, Winter 2013–2014 (2014).

13   Andrea Phillips, 'Pavilion Politics,' *Log* 20 (Fall 2010), pp. 104–115.

14   Lavin, 'Vanishing Point,' p. 219.

agency, and hence their capacity for architectural innovation.

In her 2010 essay 'Pavilion Politics,' which appeared in a special issue of *Log* dedicated to the topic of curating architecture, Phillips offers one of the most nuanced critiques of the situation to this date. The concept of the pavilion has shifted, she argues, from 'one of social experimentation to one of neat and transposable commodification.'[13] While Phillips recognizes the blatant commercialism of the Serpentine program in particular, she stops short of casting them in the pejorative. Instead, she attributes the conventionalization of recent projects to the demands of contemporary capital, and to their complicity with the politics of branded arts sectors: issues that she suggests are changing the very nature of art, architecture and their institutional relations.

By contrast, Lavin's 2012 essay 'Vanishing Point' argues powerfully that contemporary pavilion architecture has reached a 'state of self-referential exhaustion.'[14] Above all else, Lavin argues that the proliferation of pavilions is a sign of their demise as objects of cultural import. However, Lavin misses the significance of understanding the pavilions as a phenomenon. She writes:

> Today's pavilions are no longer proleptic, having lost any connection to an advanced cultural or

15   Ibid., p. 214.

historical project. Without a teleological motiva-
tion rooted in the belief that architecture's role is
to realize the zeitgeist, these 'pavilionized' buildings cannot function as an index of disciplinary
ambition for the future. The pavilion is thus
simultaneously an acutely contemporary symptom of the forces shaping our cultural landscape
and—perhaps more provocatively—an
anachronism.[15]

As with any cultural object, Lavin argues, popular
adoption has quashed the pavilion's ability to distin-
guish advanced tastes and social positions. At the
same time, it diminishes a latent capacity for experimentation and truly surprising transgressions.
Lavin's desire to restrict the pavilion to critical cultural production—always in advance of broader
architectural practice—and her lament at the loss the
pavilion's critical agency, we would like to argue
here, ignores two important issues. First, she holds
on to criticality as if it were a trans-historical measure of artistic worth. Yet, the pavilion as a type—
if it can indeed be considered as such—belongs to a
longer tradition that includes, but far exceeds, the
experimental model of modernism. Second, her
argument is predicated on a belief in another modern
idea: the teleological progress of art and architecture.
Paradoxically, in championing a modernist concept

of proleptic architecture, she effectively tries to fix the pavilion within a narrow band of its own history. Lavin overlooks the kinds of values that William Kent, for example, exercised in his garden structures in the eighteenth century, as well as the changes taking place in contemporary practice—changes that introject the concepts and categories of art and architecture differently than they had been under modernist concepts of art disciplines.

Lavin's position on the pavilion is also strongly marked by assumptions about the disciplinary integrity of architecture. However, many interesting questions arise from the fact that pavilion programs are frequently realized by visual arts institutions, creating a new institutional context for contemporary architecture. This aspect of the phenomenon was recognized in 2012 in a special issue of *Artforum* on the changing relationship between art and architecture, in which a range of contributors, Lavin amongst them, discussed the expanding instances of, and opportunities for, exchange between art and architecture. Unsurprisingly, the opinions of the contributors as to the benefits and detriments of the convergence between the two disciplines significantly differ. Whereas some radically equate art and architecture—'the premise of a division is specious' (Steven Holl)—others argue that a discussion of disciplinary relations cannot be separated from 'specific

points of interaction, such as the art institution'
(Julian Rose).[16]

There is a consensus, however, that developments within art institutions in the past decades
have had a major impact on the rapport between art
and architecture. All agree that the conventional art
museum no longer serves as the primary reference
for the critical exchange between art and architecture, since the institution has been surpassed by all
kinds of new and often temporary forms and modes
of making art public: from art fairs and biennials,
to city exhibitions (see Proposition 5). Hans Ulrich
Obrist, arguably one of the most influential figures in
creating new contexts for an exchange between art
and architecture in the past decade, goes further in
claiming the significance of these shifts in the institutional world as a determining context for the contemporary pavilion.[17] Despite the long history of
precedents recognized by others, it is Obrist's view
that: 'Julia [Peyton-Jones] invented the idea of the
pavilions in 2000 with Zaha Hadid.' Accordingly,
they arose not only out of history or the potential of
relations between architecture and the visual arts,
but out of a strategy for 'a permanent reinvention of
the institution.'[18]

16 Julian Rose et al., 'Trad-ing Spaces: A Roundtable on Art and Architecture,' *Artforum International* 51, no. 2 (2012), pp. 201, 203.

17 In 2006 he joined Peyton-Jones as co-director of the Ser-pentine Galleries, and since Peyton-Jones' departure in 2016 has assumed the role of artistic director with Jana Peel as CEO.

18 Rose et al., 'Trading Spaces,' p. 204.
Obrist introduced the Marathon event to the Serpen-tine—a 24-hour-long interview with artists, architects and other cultural figures held in association with the exhibition of the Pavilion each year.

3

That part of the success
of the Serpentine Galleries'
pavilion program lies
in its opening up of
the question of whether
architecture is art.

19   *Jamming Gears* by Richard Wilson (1996) engaged directly with obsolete parts of the building, while the 'Inside Out' (1996–1997) program exhibited a series of site-specific works outside the gallery, including a work by Tadashi Kawamata made of doors and windows taken from the building and reassembled in a free-standing sculptural arrangement on the lawn (*Relocation*, 1997).

In their recent manifestations, pavilions have frequently invoked a conversation between architecture and the visual arts. This is most clearly demonstrated in the example of the Serpentine Pavilions, and often repeated by the other pavilion programs emerging in their wake. In the case of the Serpentine, this conversation preceded, and was a catalyst for, the pavilion program, and emerged in conjunction with the renovation of the Grade II heritage listed gallery building by John Miller & Partners in 1996–1998. During this period the gallery commissioned a series of site specific artworks that took on an architectural scale.[19] To celebrate the completion of the renovation in 1998, they extended this process of in-situ commissioning to architects, inviting Seth Stein to design a temporary canopy structure as a setting for the party celebrating the reopening of the gallery.

26

The meeting of artistic and architectural processes in this moment is recognized by former director Julia Peyton-Jones as a kind of prehistory to the pavilion program, opening up the prospect of commissioning contemporary architecture in the same way as art. The continuation of the summer party tradition provided further opportunities for temporary architectural structures to be commissioned, and led to the formalization of the pavilion program just a few years later. In fact, what is designated as the inaugural pavilion by Zaha Hadid in 2000 is more correctly understood as part of these formative encounters with temporary architecture. It was only in the wake of the popularity of Hadid's pavilion that Christopher Smith, Minister for Culture Media and Sport in Tony Blair's government, helped arrange permission from the Royal Parks for the gallery to extend the timeframe of these structures and ultimately mount a recurring pavilion program in Kensington Gardens.[20]

While the Serpentine Pavilion commission gained a reputation in its early days as a form of advocacy for contemporary architecture—and despite the Serpentine Galleries' insistence on the program as an architectural commission—there are nonetheless recurring instances where the pavilions raise questions about the disciplinary boundaries of art and architecture.[21] Libeskind's 2001 pavilion

20 Jodidio, 'Interview with Julia Peyton-Jones and Hans Ulrich Obrist,' p. 9.

21 As described by Joel Robinson, the early pavilions 'reflect[ed] the architectural establishment's late embrace of the deconstructivist style as popularized by Philip Johnson in an exhibition at New York's Museum of Modern Art in 1988. In the British context, deconstructivism was enlisted as a weapon against the fairy-tale historicism of the Prince of Wales and his circle.' Joel Robinson, 'Pavilions as Public Sculpture: Serpentine Pavilions,' *World Sculpture News* 21, no. 4 (Autumn 2015), p. 33.

27

22   Libeskind's pavilion thereby established the concept of the pre-sale of the pavilion. It was eventually purchased by an unknown buyer, and loaned in 2005 to the city of Cork as part of its celebrations as the European Capital of Culture. Marina Otero Verzier, 'Tales from Beyond the Grave,' *Domus* 12 November 2012, www.domusweb.it/en/architecture/2012/11/12/tales-from-beyond-the-grave.html.

Other occasional literature on the afterlives of pavilions include: Oliver Wainwright, 'Beach Café, Billionaire's Retreat, Wedding Marquee: Second lives of the Serpentine pavilion,' *The Guardian*, 17 June 2015, www.theguardian.com/artanddesign/2015/jun/16/serpentine-pavilion-second-lives-zaha-hadid-toyo-ito-frank-gehry; Anna Winston, 'Burnt, Recycled, Sold: The Fate of 2015's Temporary Pavilions,' *Dezeen*, 14 June 2016, www.dezeen.com/2016/06/14/2015-temporary-pavilions-fate-burnt-recycled-storage-sold-serpentine-gallery-milan-expo-moma-ps1/.

23   In 2006 the Koolhaas and Balmond pavilion included a frieze by Thomas Demand, even though the pavilions are not intended to be for the display of art, which might confuse their remit to exhibit architecture. In 2012 the collaboration between Herzog & de Meuron and Ai Weiwei allowed a stretching of the usual criteria of the program—to commission architects who had not completed a building in the UK at the time of the invitation—so that this celebrated partnership, responsible for the 2008 Beijing Olympic 'Bird's Nest' stadium, could design the pavilion in the year of the London Olympics. Herzog & de Meuron had previously completed the Laban Dance School building in the UK in 2002. While they had an established working relationship with Ai Weiwei, they had not undertaken a project together in the UK at the time of the invitation.

24   Jodidio, 'Interview with Julia Peyton-Jones and Hans Ulrich Obrist,' p. 16. On the scale of Eliasson's studio, see Philip Ursprung, *Studio Olafur Eliasson: An Encyclopedia* (Cologne: Taschen, 2008); Philip Ursprung, 'Narcissistic Studio: Olafur Eliasson,' in Wouter Davidts and Kim Paice, eds., *The Fall of the Studio: Artists at Work* (Amsterdam: Valiz, 2009), pp. 163–184.

Eighteen Turns, for example, was conceived as a reproducible object—not, however, like Le Corbusier's Pavillon de l'Esprit Nouveau (1924) that was to be a model for serial architecture in the modern world, where architecture was a capacity that was instantiated in its material production—but more like a limited edition of artists prints, the sales of which would finance their construction. [22] No multiples, however, were ever made.

Subsequent pavilions have only blurred disciplinary distinctions further. In 2007, artist Olafur Eliasson took top billing in a collaboration with architect Kjetil Thorsen (Snøhetta), in one of several commissions that have paired artists with architects.[23] Peyton-Jones has explained this particular anomaly as Eliasson 'wearing his architectural hat' for this commission—a statement that highlights the degree to which Eliasson's absorption of architectural processes and techniques has become a recognized form of practice in the art world, not to mention the scale of his studio enterprise.[24] Even when disciplinary distinctions are maintained, the ambiguity between categories of art and architecture are on display: some of the most recent structures even look decidedly like art, as we argue in our sixth proposition.

Certainly, the Serpentine Pavilion program is an occasion for a conversation between art and architecture. Part of its success rests with its opening up the question: 'is architecture art?' This question succeeds in making an event, a cultural moment, a 'pavilion' if you will, precisely because it cannot be resolved or fixed. Instead—and the Serpentine program is a case in point—the pavilion opens onto all of these occasions, theories and policies, past and projected, including those where this question appears to have been answered, and that answer has not stuck.[25]

25 A more detailed analysis of the conversation between art and architecture in the history of the Serpentine Gallery Pavilions is outlined in: Susan Holden, '"To Be with Architecture Is All We ask": A Critical Genealogy of the Serpentine Pavilions,' in *Quotation, Quotation: 34th Annual Conference of the Society of Architectural Historians, Australia and New Zealand*, ed. Gevork Hartoonian and John Ting (Canberra: SAHANZ, 2017).

4

That pavilions are a demonstration of the capacity of architecture to be collected and exhibited by galleries and museums.

A largely unexamined aspect of the contemporary pavilion is its complicity with the pre-existing curatorial and exhibitionary practices of art institutions, and its latent capacity to be bought, collected and sold alongside, and in the same context as, art. Historically, museums have tended to collect representations of architecture, such as drawings and models, while fragments of buildings treated like sculpture have also found their way into various collections of art and archaeology. Likewise, period rooms have long existed in some museums and are something of a precedent for the emerging present-day practice of collecting full-scale buildings. Indeed, museums and galleries are now acquiring in-situ works of architecture with increasing aplomb: LACMA was recently announced as the beneficiary of a multi-million-dollar donation of the Sheats-

Goldstein residence designed by John Lautner. Even more conspicuous was The Met's 2013 lease of the former Whitney Museum by Marcel Breuer, occupied and newly rebranded as the Met Breuer.[26] The building has not only become a much-needed exhibition space, but also functions as part of the museum's encyclopedic collection. In other words, the building has become an exhibition of itself.

Compared to most buildings, pavilions are conducive to being collected, and the emergence of a secondary market for their purchase and sale usefully exposes moments of friction between institutional categories and recent collecting practices. In particular, this collectability needs to be read against a growing trend in museums towards the inclusion of cultural practices that, for most of the twentieth century, have been considered part of design and commercial arts—practices that include fashion, animation and architecture—and that are increasingly presented within the rising meta-category of Design. Certainly, the mild controversy that the Serpentine generates by clashing the categories of architecture and visual art needs to be understood in this wider context of a loosening of a hierarchy of culture. There is also a practical aspect to the Serpentine's program: being a *kunsthalle* it does not have a remit to collect what it commissions. Few collections of architecture other than the Vitra Campus at Weil am

26   Rosemary Willink, 'The Met Breuer: From Sculpture to Art Museum and Back Again,' in *Quotation: 34th Annual Conference of the Society of Architectural Historians, Australia and New Zealand*, ed. Gevork Hartoonian and John Ting (Canberra: SAHANZ, 2017).

27   Thordis Arrhenius et al., eds. *Place and Displacement: Exhibiting Architecture* (Zürich: Lars Müller, 2014).

Rhein have faced the problem of collecting buildings with a curatorial intent. This leaves unanswered some major questions of how architecture can be collected, and how, if architecture were to become part of the art market, acquisition and exhibition histories might affect the monetary value of works of architecture when traded on the art market (see Proposition 8).[27]

An early precedent for collection practices that include architecture is the Victoria and Albert Museum in London. Since its founding in 1852 as a 'Museum of Manufactures' it has collected and exhibited objects of utility and craft according to its founding mission to train the taste of producers and consumers. Aspects of this approach continue today in various museums of Fine Art, including the Metropolitan Museum of New York. But, while this Arts and Crafts ideology, along with its implied critique of aesthetic autonomy and hierarchy in culture, finds new purchase in present-day creative industries policy, museums have moved away from training taste as a form of civics, to follow their original idea of artistic nationalism and Romantic concepts of genius.

'Design' is now treated art-historically, with periods, authors and canonical works—its progress being evidence of the same spirits of place and time that the artworks of a people are said to exhibit. The

utility and commercial origins of most design arte-
facts have conventionally been distinguished by
lacking the freedom of the fine arts, but now design
is also defined positively by the widespread accept-
ance of the authority of the creative economy, within
which fine art museums also find themselves today.
The various architecture and design centers, which
are now a standard museum type, suppose a
collection and exhibition structure like that of a fine
art museum, but with the disciplinary distinction
between 'art' and 'design' maintained.[28] If we take
the V & A as laying out the territory of a museological
regime that incorporated art and what we now
call 'design'; then the contemporary architecture
museum would be the opposing approach—insti-
tutionalizing a disciplinary distinction with tools
common to the fine art museum. Both of these
approaches in their own way try to rationalize the
place of architecture in culture. However, the architectural pavilions that interest us here, are something
different: an introjection of architecture into visual
arts institutions. In these circumstances the institutional and disciplinary categories are set at odds
with the ideational structures of a work, or a curatorial approach, and thus ask more interesting questions. But, whether in new design museums, or
in new departments within old institutions, architectural works are treated more as objects of art than

28 The International Confed-
eration of Architectural Museums (ICAM) was founded in
1979. 'About ICAM,' ICAM,
www.icam-web.org/about.php.

29 Wouter Davidts, *Triple Bond: Essays on Art, Architecture and Museums* (Amsterdam: Valiz, 2017).

they have ever been, at the same time that art, the museum and architecture have become increasingly bound together.[29]

5

That late twentieth-century developments in art and architecture reveal an overlooked cross-disciplinary history for the pavilions.

There have been various attempts, more or less rhetorical, to define pavilions by their historical continuity or novelty. Indeed, most of the serious thought on the contemporary pavilion phenomenon gives some role to understanding them as a historically constituted building *type*. In various accounts, this history ranges from the campaign tents of medieval kings (as demonstrated by the etymological connection to the Latin *papilio)*, to eighteenth-century garden structures, nineteenth- and twentieth-century exhibitionary buildings (displaying goods and national identities), as well as twentieth-century modernist prototypes—particularly those of Le Corbusier and Mies van der Rohe. The length of these histories and their chosen threshold points support the various authors' views on the contemporary phenomenon, leaving a pervasive ambiguity in the pavilion's

30   Robinson, 'Introducing Pavilions,' p. 9.

31   Ibid., p. 7.

definition, and whether or not its highly variable historical forms constitute a unified building type.

We follow Joel Robinson's argument that the pavilion's amorphous forms, contingent functions and genealogical inconsistency elude typological categorization.[30] His suggestion that the pavilion should be understood as a 'medium' for those working at the art-architecture nexus is also persuasive.[31] But irrespective of such discursive positions, the fact that the term 'pavilion' has come to describe such a diverse range of architectural structures—from small breakfronts in a façade, to large standalone edifices (consider, for example, John Nash's palace-sized Brighton Pavilion)—is inexorable. Moreover, the conflation of the pavilion with analogous, but nonidentical, historical concepts including 'folly' and 'fabrique,' serve only to frustrate attempts at classification.

What is interesting to us is the way in which the longest chronologies of the pavilion reinforce a concept of architecture as a distinct discipline based on types which belong to it. The pavilion is then an appropriable vehicle for conspicuously expensive experiments in architectural forms and ideas, whether these are eighteenth-century concepts of wit, utopian housing, 'criticality,' or art. In contrast, those who start their histories with the social and technical experiments of modernism emphasize a concept of architecture as progressing or regressing its own internal problematics. Both of these strategies of historical contextualization are relevant, if limited by certain subjectivities. In contrast, for Obrist to date the origin of the pavilion to Peyton-Jones' commissioning of Hadid in 2000 (see Proposition 2) seems hyperbolic, and certainly it contradicts both typological and teleological accounts of the pavilion's history. However, by defining the pavilion as he does in the confrontation of architecture and the visual arts makes sense if given a more complex and nuanced history from the last decades of the twentieth century into the present.

The 'follies' of the 1980s and 1990s, a term closely associated with Bernard Tschumi, the Parc de la Villette and the theory of deconstructivism, are an obvious precedent and yet largely overlooked in the discussion of the contemporary pavilions.[32] Whether the terminological distinction of folly/pavilion is significant or not, and whether the strongly disciplinary culture of architecture in the 1990s differs from the post-medial art cultures of the present, remains to be explored. Surely, however, these recent episodes are at least as relevant as understanding the current pavilion phenomenon in terms inherited from Willian Kent or Le Corbusier.

The tendency to cast the pavilion as an archi-

32   Annalise Varghese, 'Following the Folly: Quoting, Constructing and Historicising Paper Architecture,' in *Quotation, Quotation: 34th Annual Conference of the Society of Architectural Historians, Australia and New Zealand*, ed. Gevork Hartoonian and John Ting (Canberra: SAHANZ, 2017).

37

33   Léa-Catherine Szacka, *Exhibiting Postmodernism: The 1980 Venice Architecture Biennale* (Venezia: Marsillo, 2016).

tectural type has also closed down other genealogies and histories that are important for understanding the emergence of the contemporary pavilion in the context of the visual arts institution. While both Phillips and Lavin see the present-day pavilions as the backwash and popularization of the land art and conceptual art of the 1970s, they skip over developments in the intervening decades. Of particular significance here are a set of events that occurred in the 1980s and 1990s, which commenced the process that Obrist describes wherein architecture became key to new forms of engagement with artworks and institutions. The first Venice Biennale of Architecture of 1980 was one key moment where exhibitions of architecture took on the model of art fairs and institutionalized a disciplinary distinction between architecture and visual arts.[33] However, significant exhibition practices continued to be cross-disciplinary and collaborative. In the same period a series of exhibitions involving both artists and architects were mounted, including 'Collaborations' at the Architecture League of New York (1981), 'Art and Architecture' at ICA (1983) and 'Theatergarden Bestiarium' at PS1 (1989). The differing constraints of exhibiting and collecting (see Proposition 4) continue to influence the categorization of art and architecture. At the same time, the festivalization of culture has seen a proliferation of biennales and fairs of both art and architecture, and are an important context for the pavilions that concerns us here.

The 1980s also marked the start of a new type of exhibition that, following the example of art practice in the 1960s and 1970s, left the space of the museum.[34] In so-called *extra-muros* exhibitions—including such canonical examples as Skulptur Projekte (Münster, 1977) and Chambres d'Amis (Ghent, 1986), both of which were organized by art museums—the artistic strategy of site-specificity was recuperated, appropriated and formalized by the institution into an invitation to artists to leave the museum 'together.'[35] Whereas the term site-specific initially was only used for individual art projects, it was then also applied to a new exhibition genre: the 'site-specific exhibition.'[36] Increasingly, artists were invited to present and develop work outside the space of the museum, in either a park or an urban context.

In two different respects this new form of exhibition fueled the blossoming of the contemporary phenomenon of the pavilion. First, the conditions and resources advanced by such initiatives stimulated, if not forced, artists to opt for a large-scale approach. Inevitably, artists felt compelled to produce works of an increasingly larger size, and installations of an unavoidably architectural nature, in public space.[37] Dan Graham's pavilions, which he

34 Another aspect of this history that is not well articulated is the role of post-World War II reconstruction and public art projects in the guise of garden and sculpture exhibitions. These were precursors to the 1980s site-specific sculpture exhibitions (including the International Sculpture Exhibition at Sonsbeek Park, Arnhem, and Germany's Bundesgartenschau—which lead to Documenta, and the International Garden Festivals). This immediate post-World War II history opens up an alternative context in which to understand the pavilions as a form of public art.

35 Johanne Lamoureux, 'The Museum Flat,' in *Thinking About Exhibitions*, ed. Bruce Ferguson, Reesa Greenberg, and Sandy Nairne (London: Routledge, 1996), p. 114.

36 Reesa Greenberg, 'The Exhibited Redistributed: A Case for Reassessing Space,' in *Thinking About Exhibitions*, ed. Bruce Ferguson, Reesa Greenberg, and Sandy Nairne (London: Routledge, 1996), p. 350; Mary Jane Jacob, 'Making History in Charleston,' in *Places with a Past: New Site-Specific Art at Charleston's Spoleto Festival*, eds. Mary Jane Jacob and Christian Boltanski (New York: Rizzoli 1991), p. 16.

37 This scalar increase, Lavin rightly argues, brings art inevitably closer to architecture, as it produces work that is 'so conceptually expansive that its ultimate medium is necessarily a small building.' Lavin, 'Vanishing Point,' p. 216.

39

38   Beatrice Colomina is one of the few critics to have brought the work of Dan Graham into the discourse on the contemporary pavilion: Beatriz Colombia, 'Beyond Pavilions: Architecture as a Mahine to See,' in *The Pavilion: Pleasure and Polemics in Architecture*, ed. Peter Cachola Schmal (Ostfildern: Hatje Cantz, 2009).

39   Davidts, *Triple Bond*.

developed partly out of the opportunity to exhibit at such large-scale, outdoor sculpture exhibitions, are a pertinent example.[38] Second, and of equal importance, is the resulting need for (temporary) infrastructure to support such extra-institutional events, whether staged in bucolic or urban settings. Some of these ever more took the shape of pavilions.

If the advent of the site-specific exhibition in the 1980s made art more like architecture, then the museum boom that occurred in parallel made architecture more art-like. Hans Hollein's Museum Abteiberg in Mönchengladbach (1972–1982), Richard Meier's Museum for the Decorative Arts in Frankfurt (1979–1985) and the Getty Center in LA (1984–1997) announced this trend, but it was the Guggenheim Museum's global expansion strategy under the directorship of Thomas Krens (1988–2008) that serves as a useful parallel for understanding the changing role of architecture in art museums: the proliferation of pavilions are in part an aftereffect of the trend towards architecturally designed art museums as destinations in themselves.[39] The Serpentine Pavilion commission, for example, cleverly exploits this model of leveraging the exhibitionary power of architecture (ten of the seventeen named architects or firms of the Serpentine Pavilions have been Pritzker Prize winners). Rather than providing new venues to show expanding collections, the Serpentine Pavilions have become beacons for programs of events. They nevertheless amount to a similar kind of brand expansion through the display of contemporary architecture, evident in the way Peyton-Jones has described them as 'the new "wing" that we create every year [which] is the exhibition itself.'[40]

The difficulties faced by museums in expanding and franchising has been accompanied by a surge of interest in pavilions, as institutions have realized they offer an expedient way to get architecture without 'hav[ing] to pay for plumbing.'[41] The Guggenheim, for example, has now devolved their expansion strategy to include pavilions (Guggenheim BMW Pavilion, Atelier Bow-Wow, 2014) and architectural competitions held without any commitment to realizing a new building (Guggenheim Helsinki, 2014).

It is these recent histories, more than the familiar ones of long disciplinary coherence or twentieth-century avant-gardism, that are needed to understand the contemporary pavilion.

40 Jodidio, 'Interview with Julia Peyton-Jones and Hans Ulrich Obrist,' p. 14.

41 Lavin, 'Vanishing Point,' p. 216.

6

That the concepts of disciplinary differentiation that play out in pavilions have themselves become a topic or material for architecture and art.

42 L.E. Shiner, *The Invention of Art: A Cultural History* (Chicago: University of Chicago Press, 2001); Paul Oskar Kristeller, 'The Modern System of the Arts,' in *Renaissance Thought and the Arts: Collected Essays* (Princeton, NJ: Princeton University Press, 1990); John Macarthur and Andrew Leach, 'Architecture, Disciplinarity, and the Arts: Considering the Issues,' in *Architecture, Disciplinarity, and the Arts*, ed. Andrew Leach and John Macarthur (Ghent, Belgium: A&S books, 2009).

The exchanges between art and architecture that occasion the pavilion phenomenon also need be understood in a wider context of interdisciplinary relations between art and architecture and the structures that purport to explain this. The concept of an art discipline goes back to medieval guilds and further into the classical past. Philosophers in the eighteenth century such as Diderot and d'Alembert, laid over these ancient groupings the idea that the differing arts were divisions or departments of 'Art'—an 'art-as-such'—that paired with nature in addressing an innate aesthetic faculty.[42] They devised lists and diagrams that showed how art disciplines were neighbors to one another, formed hierarchies, and added up these constituent parts to a total conception of art.

Since then, there have been two competing

structures by which we might understand disciplines and their interrelations. We might call these the 'disciplinary' and the 'aesthetic.' The latter structure supposes that there is art-as-such that answers to an aesthetic faculty. It would follow, then, that the pavilions and wider developments in contemporary art and architecture might be understood as the rise of new interdisciplines, that will replace, or sit alongside, older unities like architecture and sculpture.[43] On the other hand, we might think that art-as-such and aesthetics are retrospective analytic categories that are merely speculation laid over the concrete, historically situated disciplines, in which case we could see the pavilions as negotiating the differentiation of art and architecture on each occasion. This disciplinary concept has been the dominant stream in both architecture and the visual arts in the later twentieth century. The persistence of past categories nonetheless has an effect in the present. While it looks like there is an ongoing question about whether categories are being brought together or kept apart (synthesis of the arts vs systems of the arts), the real question is more about temporal synchronicity. In the present it seems that the administrative categories are out of step with practice, and that they are developing at different speeds.

It is significant that the pavilions play out aporias in aesthetic theory from the eighteenth century but,

43 It is possible to take a long historical view of interdisciplinary practice. See: Joseph Rykwert, *The Judicious Eye: Architecture Against the Other Arts* (Chicago: University of Chicago, 2008). And cf. the more recent chronology of Jane Rendell's concept of 'critical spatial practice': Jane Rendell, *Art and Architecture: A Place Between* (London and New York: I.B. Tauris, 2007).

43

44   Rosalind Krauss, 'Sculpture in the Expanded Field,' *October* 8 (1979).

45   Ila Berman and Douglas Burnham, *Expanded Field: Architectural Installation Beyond Art* (Novato, CA: AR+D Publishing, 2016).

46   Isabelle Loring Wallace and Nora Wendl, *Contemporary Art about Architecture* (Burlington: Ashgate, 2013).

47   John Macarthur, 'The Semblance of Use: Function and Aesthetics in Contemporary Art Pavilions and the Longer History of Ornamental Buildings,' in *Quotation Quotation: 34th Annual Conference of the Society of Architectural Historians, Australia and New Zealand*, ed. Gevork Hartoonian and John Ting (Canberra: SAHANZ, 2017).

again, the relevant context for the current inquiry is more recent. This begins in the 1970s and 1980s with artists such as Dan Graham, Gordon Matta-Clark, Daniel Buren, Mary Miss, and SITE working with the built environment, and with architects. Rosalind Krauss' 1979 article 'Sculpture in the Expanded Field' crystallized how questions of disciplinary differentiation were arising in practice at this time.[44] Krauss supposes that art disciplines are no longer founded on essential aspects of their media, nor the unfolding problematics of their own history. Rather, disciplines define themselves through mutual opposition, each exemplifying what the other is not. The widely reproduced semiotic square diagram that Krauss used to explain a sophisticated disciplinary account of the arts has since become a landmark that practices orient themselves from.[45]

If these aforementioned practices can be said to act on architecture and buildings as a kind of critical material—a material in the world—then a shift can be observed in the 1990s. Since then, a strand of contemporary art has taken the disciplines of architecture and design as its topos.[46] Allan Wexler's logical but irrational buildings, Jorge Pardo's designer chic, and Andrea Zittel's play on the modernist project of reforming everyday life, are all pitched as architecture in a parallel world.[47] At the same time, Thomas Demand and Callum Morton have made

44

explicit commentary on architecture as a cultural form, while Ai Weiwei and Olafur Eliasson have worked on more conventional architectural projects. The built environment also makes an obvious territory for the strategies of relational aesthetics employed by artists interested in the problematic of participatory works—such artists as Rirkrit Tiravanija, Thomas Hirschhorn and Jeanne van Heeswijk. Utility is one point around which the disciplines differentiate—the slight and even negligent relation that the Serpentine's Pavilions have to their function as coffee bars and so on, is the inverse of the way that utility becomes a means of participation in much relational art.[48] Equally strange inversions include the 2015 Turner Prize going to the architectural collaborative, Assemble, for a body of work that looks like relational aesthetics discovering social utility, but which, in architectural discourse, appears as nostalgia for the participatory design of the 1960s and 1970s. Within this history there is also a trajectory of architecture engaging with artists and art practice through collaborations, and a growing number of architects exhibiting work in gallery settings in the 1980s and 1990s.[49] Further, some recent critical architectural practice involves the representation of architecture, such as Robbrecht en Daem's temporary 1:1 reconstruction of Ludwig Mies van der Rohe's Golf Club House at Krefeld, which is

48   On the dysfunctionality of the pavilions see: Marina Otero Verzier, 'Fair Trade: Architecture and Coffee at the Serpentine Gallery Pavilions,' *Avery Review* 9 (2015).

49   Consider, for example, the exhibition *para-site* at MoMA in 1989 by Elizabeth Diller and Ricardo Scofidio.

45

50   Maarten Liefooghe, 'Criti-
cal Performance: Robbrecht en
Daem's 1:1 Model of Mies' Kre-
feld Golf Club Project' (unpub-
lished article manuscript,
Ghent, 2016), based on the
conference paper 'Replicas as
Critical Architectural Perfor-
mances: Mies 1:1 Golf Club
Project' presented at the 68th
Annual Conference of the Soci-
ety of Architectural Historians,
Chicago, April 15–19, 2015. See
also: Maarten Liefooghe and
Stefaan Vervoort, 'Een reveler-
end gesprek: de figuren van
Thomas Schütte in Het Huis van
Robbrecht & Daem,' De Witte
Raaf 158 (July–August 2012).

51   Rose et al., 'Trading
Spaces,' p. 202.

52   Hal Foster, The Art-Architecture Complex (London: Verso,
2011), viii.

somehow not building, but takes its mode from installation art.[50]

Hal Foster has argued that the relation of art and architecture is historically determined in a way that leaves but two options that match against what we have called the 'aesthetic' and the 'disciplinary': 'There's a *Gesamtkunstwerk* model—one of combination; and a differential model—one of co-articulation.'[51] The case of the Serpentine shows a clear preference for co-articulation, or a 'differential specificity' of the disciplines. But elsewhere Foster points to a third possibility. He writes that, 'not long ago, a near prerequisite for vanguard architecture was an engagement with theory; lately it has become an acquaintance with art.'[52] We can see an aspect of this disciplinary differentiation and Foster's 'acquaintance with art' in the Serpentine program, particularly in the quotation and translation of artworks and concepts by architects. This intricate 'practice' draws the architects closer to the visual arts at the same time that the structure of referencing and citation guarantees them a distance.

Asserting the disciplinary integrity of architecture in the pavilions seems to require a fine balance of bringing it as close as possible to the visual arts in conceptual terms, and often in its formal qualities, while maintaining disciplinary differences through the reification of the disciplinary categories. But it is also the case that the pavilions reference particular artworks, often without comment or citation. Sou Fujimoto's 2013 pavilion ostensibly refers to Sol LeWitt's white cubic spatial constructions,[53] while Smiljan Radić's 2014 structure was conspicuous not only for its formal resemblance to Frederick Kiesler's *Endless House* (1947–1960) but also to the sculpture *Rock on Top of Another Rock* by Fischli/Weiss that was simultaneously exhibited on the lawn of the Gallery. We could also add to this list the Koolhaas-Balmond pavilion of 2006, which takes up the unconstructed works of Yves Klein's architecture of air and fire, as well as selgascano's 2015 pavilion, seemly inspired by Jorge Pardo's *Oliver, Oliver, Oliver* of 2004. Is this referencing or mimesis? Has art become nature for the 'art' of architecture? Or is this a kind of cultural aggression in the mode of appropriation art? If, in 2011, Foster observed that references to art had replaced 'theory' in architectural discourse, this process seems to have gone through another turn and artworks and art itself have now become a material of architectural practice.

The second aspect of this interdisciplinary relation is that the quotation and referencing of artworks in architectural works, and *vice versa*, not only connotes the relations the disciplines have with one another, but a further relation by making the system of differentiated disciplines a kind of topic. Krauss'

53 Joel Robinson has likened Fujimoto's pavilion to a specific object of Donald Judd: 'the stated intention of conjuring the image of a cloud verged on kitsch, when what really came to mind here was a bastardized take on Donald Judd's notion of the 'specific object'—i.e. a minimalist version of a climbing frame for toddlers.' Robinson, 'Pavilions as Public Sculpture,' p. 34.

54   Anthony Vidler, *Architecture Between Spectacle and Use* (Sterling and Francine Clark Art Institute: Williamstown, MA; Yale University Press: New Haven, CT, 2008); Spyros Papapetros and Julian Rose, *Retracing the Expanded Field: Encounters Between Art and Architecture* (Cambridge, MA: MIT Press, 2014).

diagram of the expanded field has been taught in architecture and art schools for four decades, and has been historicized and explicitly turned to the question of architecture by the likes of Anthony Vidler, Spyros Papapetros and Julian Rose.[54] The disciplinarity question has itself become kind of material for practice. Something like art-as-such returns in the actual organization of pedagogy except that it is now connoted in inter-medial practice rather than authorized by an aesthetic faculty of mind. The differences between Krauss' diagram and that of Diderot and d'Alembert in the *Encyclopedia* begin to fade as theoretical and philosophical arguments about the whole-ness or collected-ness of art are appropriated into practice.

That pavilions raise the recurring question of whether the aesthetic experience of buildings is like, or unlike, the experience of artworks.

The Serpentine Galleries operate with an understanding that their annual pavilions are inherently approachable, breaking down institutional barriers through their placement in the grounds of Kensington Gardens. But this physical accessibility is reinforced by another common belief that the aesthetic experience of architecture is not only less demanding than that of the visual arts, but also more direct and less mediated by cultural knowledge. By virtue of its functionality and practicality, architecture has the advantage that once it is understood (for example, that the pavilion provides a bar, shelter, or seating) that this is sufficient to begin enjoying a direct sensory experience. Any understanding of the complexities of architectural discourse is a supplement to this immediate aesthetic contract, or so the story goes. In contrast, many contemporary artists

55   For an eloquent rebuttal of the return of beauty in contemporary art see Alexander Alberro, 'Beauty Knows No Pain,' Art Journal 63, no. 3 (2004), pp. 36–43.

56   Note the photogenic quality of many contemporary pavilions and the interrelationship between the pavilion phenomenon and the new image economy associated with the popular sharing of digital architectural photography.

57   Manfredo Tafuri, Architecture and Utopia: Design and Capitalist Development, trans. Barbara Luigia La Penta (Cambridge, MA: MIT Press, 1976).

follow the logic of the anti-aesthetic, questioning beauty and sensory experience as a basis for art. In their opposition to a traditional account of art as reconciling us with the world in the immediacy of aesthetic experience, they tend to disturb and critique our relation to the world instead.[55] Displays of contemporary architecture at the Serpentine have one role in bridging this gap between aesthetic and anti-aesthetic accounts of art, between the sensuality of summertime in the Gardens, and the demanding critical encounters awaiting in the Galleries. While equally progressive, and promising conceptual depths, the pavilions are more immediately present, less demanding of existing disciplinary competency, and more akin to the traditional appreciation of art objects that ends in an experience rather than a concept, and indeed an experience that seems already formed for dissemination in social media.[56] However effective this may be for audience engagement strategies at institutions such as the Serpentine, and for contemporary architecture as whole, it lies over a longer history, and twists the idea of what a work of architecture is in a complex way.

Modernism in architecture was characterized by what Manfredo Tafuri has called the 'crisis of the object' of the late 1920s and 1930s.[57] The constructivist strand of architectural modernism disavowed the making of unique objects. Architecture then

50

became a set of aesthetic ideas and a constructive capacity of which material buildings were mere tokens of a power to transform the whole of the built environment.[58] To the extent that architecture considered itself an art, it could be characterized as the art that did not result in artworks. The experience of a modernist work of architecture was supposed not to be the experience of a particular building, but rather of the building as a mere instance of how socio-political forces had been marshalled and channeled by architectural concepts. Hence, early twentieth-century avant-garde architecture makes an interesting parallel to Michael Fried's charge of 'theatricality' against minimalist or literalist art of the 1960s.[59] Fried's complaint, that the minimalist espousal of mundane objecthood perverted the graceful instantaneousness of the modernist art object, is a charge that could equally be put to architectural modernism in its 'critique of the object.' For Fried, art was reduced to theatre when the unique temporality of the aesthetic encounter with the art object became merely a way of experiencing affect or sensation. Modernist architectural aesthetics has largely been this kind of anthropopathy: the building positions and moves the subject to create affects, and the architecture lay there, in its perceived affects, rather than the built instantiation. Because of this history, to imply today that architecture is an art-

58 Manfredo Tafuri, 'Toward a Critique of Architectural Ideology,' in *Architectural Theory since 1968*, ed. K. Michael Hays (Cambridge, MA: MIT Press, 1998 [1969]), pp. 6–35.

59 Michael Fried, 'Art and Objecthood,' *Artforum* 5, no. 10 (1967); Michael Fried, *Art and Objecthood: Essays and Reviews* (Chicago: University of Chicago Press, 1998).

51

work, has strange resonances.

    The architecture committed to Tafuri's critique of the object is long past in these days of starchitects and iconic buildings. The situation of the pavilions in visual arts venues is thus quite paradoxical. They are said to be advertisements for architectural capacity as in the day of high-modernist proleptic exhibitions of a future architecture (the task in which they fail, according to Lavin). But, in their venue in visual arts institutions, in the requirement for novelty that they fulfil, and in the engagement of a wider public that their easy aestheticization is said to enable, they seem to be the very model of a traditional artwork. They could be seen to offer what Fried required of an artwork: a 'presentness,' which much art since minimalism stands in critique of. This, however, is not the case. It is an illusion caused by architecture having yet to think through the friction between an aesthetics of sense and the histories of the arts.

That pavilions are an index of the changing relation of cultural and monetary value, which is shifting the plane on which architecture and the visual arts meet.

The Serpentine's pavilion program is also evidence that it is becoming harder to maintain the invisible wall that separates cultural and economic value. If the epitome of art since the Enlightenment was portable panel painting—indifferent to its location; produced by artists who were autonomous in the sense of being unsalaried by a patron; offering their work on an open market, the only criterion of which was aesthetic value—then, in contrast, architecture looked much more constrained. It was commissioned largely to improve the commercial value of land, fixed to a site and not tradable in itself, and often defined by a pre-existing function. This, indeed, is still a common reasoning for excluding architecture from art, despite the long history of architecture joining painting and sculpture in art history text books, and despite the commissioning

60   Lucy R. Lippard, *Six Years: The Dematerialization of the Art Object from 1966 to 1972* (London: Studio Vista, 1973).

and patronage structures of historical and contemporary visual art. For architecture to be seen as too commercial to achieve the material or aesthetic autonomy of art, we would need to also put out of consideration the speculation in the monetary value of art works in which both commercial galleries and public collecting institutions are engaged.

On the one hand, this non-artistic status is what makes the frisson of bringing architecture into the gallery. In another light, pavilion programs weaken the contrast of commercial and cultural value. The pavilions are more art-like in being relatively functionless, often portable, commissioned by visual arts curators explicitly for the auteur status of the architects. Many, including the Serpentine Pavilions, are pre-sold into a nascent secondary art market for architectural works. At the same time, the contemporary artworks descended from the traditions of painting and sculpture, are more building-like in their scale and procurement, being frequently commissioned by curators and conceived in relation to a specific gallery space, all without undermining the art market as once might have been thought.[60]

When, traditionally, we think of the visual arts as autonomous with a secondary social value, we ignore the large market for art and the financial speculation that happens there. The export value of paintings and sculpture from the UK in 2014 was

54

£2.6 billion.[61] While the curatorial decisions made in exhibiting and collecting art might be made in the disinterested terms of aesthetic and art historical judgment, they nevertheless are creating the value differentials that make trading and speculating in artworks possible. While the idea of commercial intelligence in the art market goes back to Roger de Piles' list of hot artists, Phillips has recently shown how modern databases have vastly accelerated the determination of art by the art market.[62] She earlier described the part that pavilions play in the commodification of art in neoliberal times.[63] That architecture is practiced on a commercial basis that involves land speculation is a commonplace and there are not the same social constraints in speaking of the cultural value of a building and its value as real estate, as when speaking of a painting and its price. The Serpentine Galleries' four 'Summer Houses' in 2016, and the fact that they are for sale by the real estate agency The Modern House while being a kind of art, are part of the way in which the curtain is being drawn back on the fungibility of art.[64]

Of course, there are numerous precedents for the exhibition and trade of architecture, from nineteenth-century period rooms to the late twentieth-century emergence of a market for architectural drawings exhibited and sold through commercial galleries.[65] In the contemporary context, however,

61 This is equivalent to around 25% of the UK's creative exports. By comparison, the export of film and television is valued at around £343 million. Architectural drawings were a mere £91 million. DCMS, 'Official Statistics: DCMS Sectors Economic Estimates 2016.'

62 Roger de Piles, *The Art of Painting, and the Lives of the Painters: Containing, a Compleat Treatise of Painting, Designing, and the Use of Prints: ... Done from the French of Monsieur de Piles. To which is added, an essay towards an English-School ...* (London: Printed for J. Nutt, 1706); Andrea Phillips, 'Devaluation,' *Parse* 2 (2017), pp. 107–119.

63 Phillips, 'Pavilion Politics.'

64 The Modern House, www.themodernhouse.com.

65 Jordan Kauffman, 'Architecture in the Art Market: The Max Protetch Gallery,' *Journal of Architectural Education* 70, no. 2 (2016), pp. 257–268.

66 More recently, the Serpentine Galleries has produced limited edition objects for sale in conjunction with the Serpentine Pavilions, including a steel module sculpture by Fujimoto, and signed, limited edition digital prints of models for the selgascano pavilion.

67 ArtFacts.Net, www.artfacts.net.

the pavilion signals a new and conspicuous degree of fungibility. Again, the Serpentine Pavilions offer key examples: they are typically pre-sold to collectors and architectural enthusiasts to help offset the cost of their construction. Moreover, the addition of the 'Summer Houses' to the 2016 program, on sale for fixed prices of £95,000 and £125,000, foregrounded the commercial potential for architecture as a collectible commodity that could appreciate in value.[66] The aforementioned collection of built works of architecture by major institutions, such as LACMA and the Met, therefore, is related not only to the traditions of collecting period rooms, but also to the more immediate history of an emerging market for full-scale works of architecture.

While it is well known that art auction houses link the purchasing decisions of private collectors to the value that public collections and exhibitions add to the monetary value of a work, the logic of a market exchanging art-historical value for monetary value sits unevenly over architectural materials whether these are drawings, fragments or whole buildings. In this respect, it is curious to note that *Artfacts*, a commercial site offering information for speculators in the art market, lists architects alongside visual artists.[67] However, public galleries also rely on statistics, largely visitor numbers, as proxies for their social value when requesting funding from government or philanthropists. Thus, the *Art Newspaper*'s ranking of the Serpentine Pavilions on attendance is another measure that converts architecture to money.[68] While there have been resales of some Serpentine Pavilions, it is unclear if this is yet a secondary market. What is more clear, however, is that the pavilions' pre-sale to finance their construction, and the gallery's insistence that the program is off-set by corporate and private philanthropy and in-kind support speaks to another aspect of commercialization. That is, the increasing reliance of public institutions on philanthropy, and the exchange of real and symbolic capital in the circumstance that philanthropists are also collectors.[69]

If architecture is becoming more 'arty' because of the art market, it is also useful to observe that it has retreated from its professional status.[70] In many nations architecture has a legal status as a registered profession, like law and medicine. Professionalization supposes a division of values between the regulated provision of a particular expertise for the public good and the payment for this service.[71] If architects, like medicos, had produced an effective cartel over the price for architectural services, and if the public believed in the value of their expertise, the discipline might have had a kind of universal provision of space standards like a national health service. But this is not the case. Architecture becoming more

68 José da Silva, Javier Pes, and Emily Sharpe, 'Visitor Figures 2016: Christo Helps 1.2 Million People to Walk on Water,' *The Art Newspaper*, 28 March 2017, http://theartnewspaper.com/news/visitor-figures-2016:-christo-helps-1.2-million-people-to-walk-on-water.

69 A further parallel is in the rise of publicly accessible museum quality private collections.

70 This situation has been noted by Robinson in relation to the art pavilion phenomenon: 'should it not be asked what kind of decadence has befallen architecture when it is being made to sit embarrassingly idle [on display as a pavilion] instead of providing affordable housing, functional schools or hospitals, and other fundamental services?' Robinson, 'Pavilions as Public Sculpture,' p. 32.

71 Architects in various nations campaigned for this cartel status in the early twentieth century by explicitly eschewing claims to artistic status in order to gain legal protection. Generally this was not achieved until the late 1920s and 1930s, which is to say after the high points of modernism in architecture and the visual arts. See: Thomas Graham Jackson and Richard Norman Shaw, *Architecture: Profession or an Art: Thirteen Short Essays on the Qualifications and Training of Architects* (London: John Murray, 1892); Mark Crinson and Jules Lubbock, *Architecture: Art or Profession? Three Hundred Years of Architectural Education in Britain* (Manchester: Manchester University Press, 1994).

72 David Joselit, *After Art* (Point: Essays on Architecture) (Princeton, NJ: Princeton University Press, 2013).

'arty' should be seen in this wider context of the production of values, and programs such as the Serpentine's reflect wider differentiation of the value of architecture in professional fee competition and the favorable financing arrangements available to developers employing prestige architects.

David Joselit has argued that artworks have become fungible commodities of international trade and arbitrage like bushels of wheat or pork bellies.[72] While such a situation is not quite achieved, and social-cultural resistance to commodification is not yet overcome, it is also the case that architecture cannot be absolutely fungible, despite the trade in drawings and exceptional buildings, because of the markets for property and professional services have different constraints and dynamics. Yet the increasing proximity of architecture and art in exhibitions and in commerce, provides an image of the 'invisible hand' that is moving cultural and monetary values closer together.

9

That the pavilions show some of the problems and limits in measuring and governing the cultural economy.

There is now a well-established set of administrative categories that define architecture and the visual arts within the cultural economy, and this is the field in which the homology or differentiation of cultural and economic values is being fought out. In 1998, Chris Smith, the Minister for the Department of Culture, Media and Sport (who helped gain permission for the Serpentine Pavilion program from Royal Parks)[73] published the 'Creative Industries Mapping Documents.'[74] DCMS' report provided a methodology for measuring the economic value of creativity from the old cultural forms of the visual and performing arts, to publishing and broadcast media, popular music, and new forms of creativity in software design.

Since the turn of the century, in the life span of the Serpentine Pavilions program, measuring

73 The parallel emergence of the Serpentine Pavilion program and creative industries policy in the UK has not been lost on Joel Robinson, as evident in his description of the art pavilion: 'The art pavilion is, if one wants to be really unfairly cynical, the creative industries' version of the billboard, even if the list of sponsors are more discreetly presented, with a quiet rather than brash vulgarity.' Robinson, 'Pavilions as Public Sculpture,' p. 31.

74 Department for Digital, Culture, Media & Sport, 'Creative Industries Mapping Documents 1998' (London: UK Government, DCMS, 1998), www.gov.uk/government/publications/creative-industries-mapping-documents-1998 .

75 For instance, the UK's creative economy was worth £83.1 billion per annum in 2014 (or £9.6 million per hour) and grew 37.5% (or double the rate of the economy as a whole) from 2008 to 2014. See: Department for Digital, Culture, Media & Sport, 'Official Statistics: DCMS Sectors Economic Estimates 2016' (UK Government, DCMS, 2016), www.gov.uk/government/statistics/dcms-sectors-economic-estimates-2016.

76 See for instance: Tony Bennett, *Culture: A Reformer's Science* (St Leonards, N.S.W.: Allen & Unwin, 1998) and *Making Culture, Changing Society* (London and New York: Routledge, 2013); Terry Flew, *The Creative Industries: Culture and Policy* (Los Angeles, CA: SAGE, 2012); Stuart Cunningham, *Hidden Innovation: Policy, Industry and the Creative Sector* (Brisbane: University of Queensland Press, 2013).

previously ineffable cultural and creative values in monetary terms has become of international economic significance, with a standard set of collection categories agreed through UNESCO's Framework for Cultural Statistics. The growth of a nation's creative economy is often seen as a proxy for its level of innovation and shift to a knowledge economy.[75] It is these kinds of measures that are changing cultural administration and culture as a whole. Much of the conceptual background for the idea of the creative economy arose in academic cultural studies that sought to recognize popular cultural forms. Such studies saw culture as a realm of politics or a means of governance, and brought with them a prejudice against the elitism of the traditional high arts, and against the distinction of an elite aesthetic sensibility from popular enjoyments.[76] The idea of a creative economy that spans from cultural forms like opera to creative commercial endeavors like game design, aims to be inclusive for ethico-political reasons. More pragmatically, however, it operates as a means for governments to meter public funding and to identify where this can be leveraged into wider economic returns in the real monetary economy. The terms 'creative' and 'cultural' mark a kind of war of positions where a largely British and Australian usage of 'creative industries' (where the discourse originated) is challenged by a largely European commitment to the separation of 'culture' as a sphere of human endeavor outside the money economy.[77] Both for its values and its effects in practice this kind of governing through culture and creativity has increasingly come under attack.[78]

The DCMS mapping, which continues to be developed, and the UNESCO 'cultural domains,' separate architecture and the visual arts decisively. There has been no commentary on the how these categorizations affect architecture, and none on the surprisingly contrary currents demonstrated in cultural institutions and practice that make architecture converge strongly with the visual arts, while public policy pushes them to opposite poles of the creative economy. It seems generally assumed in the study of the cultural economy that architecture's commercial nature means that it is in direct contact with popular taste, without the baggage and the subsidies afforded to the elite arts. But the self-evident facts are that architecture happens through the patronage of government, large corporations and the kind of individuals who own yachts and buy contemporary art.[79]

The logic of the categories that produce this confusion is not one of policy-making but it nevertheless has policy effects.[80] The categories are intended to be purely a means of administration, thus they merely repeat commonplaces about architecture and art, but ones that well predate the concepts at play in

77 Toby Miller, 'From Creative to Cultural Industries: Not all Industries are Cultural, and No Industries are Creative,' *Cultural Studies* 23, no. 1 (2009); David Hesmondhalgh, *The Cultural Industries*, 2nd ed. (London and Thousand Oaks, CA: Sage, 2007); Nicholas Garnham, 'From Cultural to Creative Industries: An Analysis of the Implications of the "Creative Industries" Approach to Arts and Media Policy Making in the United Kingdom,' *International Journal of Cultural Policy* 11, no. 1 (2005); Mark Banks and Justin O'Connor, 'After the Creative Industries,' *International Journal of Cultural Policy* 15, no. 4 (2009); Justin O'Connor, 'After the Creative Industries: Cultural Policy in Crisis,' *Law, Social Justice and Global Development Journal* 20 (2016).

78 Robert Hewison, *Cultural Capital: The Rise and Fall of Creative Britain* (London: Verso, 2014); Justin O'Connor, 'After the Creative Industries: Cultural Policy in Crisis,' *Journal of Law, Social Justice & Global Development* no. 1 (2016), pp. 2–18. Peter Osborne. '"Whoever Speaks of Culture Speaks of Administration as Well": Disputing Pragmatism in Cultural Studies,' *Cultural Studies* 20, no. 1 (2006), pp. 33–47.

79 John Macarthur, 'Architecture, HEAT and the Government of Culture,' in *Architecture, Institutions and Change: 32nd Annual Conference of the Society of Architectural Historians, Australia and New Zealand*, ed. Paul Hogben and Judith O'Callaghan (Sydney: SAHANZ, 2015).

80 A case in point is the development in the state of Victoria, Australia of the Victorian Design Program. The program is to be delivered by the State's premier art gallery, the National Gallery of Victoria (NGV), as a flagship of 'Creative State: Victoria's first creative industries strategy, 2016–2020,' a policy developed by the new Creative Victoria (formerly Arts Victoria). 'Creative Victoria,' Creative Victoria, http://archive.creative.vic.gov.au/News/News/2016/New_Creative_Victoria_website_launched; 'Creative State,' Creative Victoria, http://creative.vic.gov.au/about/creative-state; Linda Cheng, 'NGV to host major new Victorian Design Program,' *Architecture AU*, 16 December 2016, http://architectureau.com/articles/ngv-to-host-major-new-victorian-design-program/; 'Creative Victoria'; 'Creative State.'

81   It also has parallels with
the 'expanded field' diagrams
that, following Krauss, have
become a staple of art theory, as
discussed in Proposition 6.

contemporary cross-disciplinary practice. The categories of the creative economy are made from much older concepts of the distinction of liberal or autonomous art from forms of culture practiced commercially. Architecture is said in the U N E S C O Framework to be a creative service along with fashion, graphics and advertising. On the concentric circles model of the industries, the visual arts are a 'core cultural expression,' while architecture lies three rings further out as a 'related industry.'

This systematization and hierarchical valuing of the arts is very similar to the attempts at ordering the arts under aesthetic principles that go back to the eighteenth century.[81] Except that, in many places, the values are reversed. Architecture is a better creative industry than the visual arts not only because in economic terms it is nearly the size of the whole of the traditional arts of literature, music, drama, and the visual arts; but the more so because it does not, as they do, rely on public subsidy. In other words, it is not a 'rent-seeker' distorting the proper functioning of the creative economy. Here, there is something like a reversal of Kant's requirement for disinterestedness in making an aesthetic judgment. Architecture, thought to be commercial, has no 'interest' in shaping culture in the way that the visual and performing arts do in defending their subsidies.

Architecture is the very model of a creative

industry. It is regularly exchanging apparently intangible cultural values with hard currency. At the same time, with its longer history as an art, it is known for managing the parallel values of individual aesthetic preferences and national cultural identification. It is also the case that the whole discourse and politics of the creative economy relies on advertising, software design and architecture in order to reach a significant overall size and economic importance, when traditional visual arts have a relatively smaller stake in such calculations. In the U K, architecture is close in size to the whole of the visual and performing art.[82] Thus the arguments for government attention to cultural activities such as visual arts galleries and collections now rest very heavily on commercial creativity, including architecture.

The current convergence of art and architecture production, and the audience for the pavilion phenomenon are, of course, at the fringe of architecture as a creative industry, but this is another point where disciplinary categories and concepts, and with that practice and institutions, seem to be out of historical sequence. With the pavilions we can see how aesthetic concepts that go back as far as the eighteenth century have become both a site for new cultural practices and new administrative categories that fail to capture those practices. Certainly, the pavilions could be read as metonymic of the rapid shift in the

82   The whole of the visual and performing arts are only 6.5% of the UK's creative economy, architecture is 5%. DCMS, 'Official Statistics' 2016.

government of culture—one that is fast pulling culture values into the terms of the economy. Conversely, pavilions also evidence how the increasing prominence of the creative economy is bringing architecture back into the realm of cultural policy. Thus, they demonstrate not only the transformation of architecture through concepts of art, but that the policy direction for the visual arts is to become more like architecture. While the discourse on the contemporary pavilion has largely been concerned with the conditions under which the pavilions ask the rhetorical question 'is architecture art?' they could also be taken to be asking 'what kind of industry is art?'

Coda

If the pavilions have become something of a commonplace of present day architectural culture, they do not have to be the kind of cliché that stops thought. The intention of these 'Pavilion Propositions' has been to examine how the complex and diverging strands of concepts, practices and institutional interests are, in fact, not so easily fixed within a single, reductive idea of the pavilion, which now appears so self-evident, easily appropriated, and stamped out in increasing numbers. We have also proposed that there is a critical potential in reverse engineering the pavilion into these conceptual problems, histories, categorizing actions and institutional interests, which it gives a semblance of having been resolved. However, the ongoing growth and variety of pavilion programs are opportunities for further critical thought on the kinds of questions that our rhetorical propositions raise. While there can be no useful answer to the question of whether architecture is an art, the points where this question continues to arise are places where we can witness the shaping of the concept of architecture in the wider cultural sphere.

1   That the proliferation of pavilions is a symptom of changes in the cultural field that are affecting the concept of architecture.

2   That assessments of the pavilion phenomenon need to account for the relation of architecture and the visual arts.

3   That part of the success of the Serpentine Galleries' pavilion program lies in its opening up of the question of whether architecture is art.

4   That pavilions are a demonstration of the capacity of architecture to be collected and exhibited by galleries and museums.

5   That late twentieth-century developments in art and architecture reveal an over-looked cross-disciplinary history for the pavilions.

6   That the concepts of disciplinary differentiation
     that play out in pavilions have themselves
     become a topic or material for architecture
     and art.
7   That pavilions raise the recurring question of
     whether the aesthetic experience of buildings is
     like, or unlike, the experience of artworks.
8   That pavilions are an index of the changing rela-
     tion of cultural and monetary value, which is
     shifting the plane on which architecture and the
     visual arts meet.
9   That the pavilions show some of the problems
     and limits in measuring and governing the cul-
     tural economy.

'About ICAM.' ICAM. www.icam-web.org/about.php.

ArchDaily. www.archdaily.com.

Arrhenius, Thordis, Mari Lending, Wallis Miller, and
  Jérémie Michael McGowen, eds. *Place and
  Displacement: Exhibiting Architecture.* Zürich: Lars
  Müller, 2014.

ArtFacts.Net. www.artfacts.net.

Banks, Mark, and Justin O'Connor. 'After the Creative
  Industries.' *International Journal of Cultural Policy* 15,
  no. 4 (2009), pp. 365–373.

Bennett, Tony. *Culture: A Reformer's Science.* St Leonards,
  N.S.W.: Allen & Unwin, 1998.

———. *Making Culture, Changing Society.* London and New
  York: Routledge, 2013.

Bergdoll, Barry. 'The Pavilion and the Expanded
  Possibilities of Architecture.' In *The Pavilion: Pleasure
  and Polemics in Architecture.* Edited by Peter Cachola
  Schmal, pp. 12–33. Ostfildern: Hatje Cantz, 2009.

Berman, Ila, and Douglas Burnham. *Expanded Field:
  Architectural Installation Beyond Art.* Novato, CA:

AR+D Publishing, 2016.

Cheng, Linda. 'Ngv to Host Major New Victorian Design Program.' *Architecture AU*. Published electronically 16 December 2016. http://architectureau.com/articles/ngv-to-host-major-new-victorian-design-program/.

Cocozza, Paula. 'Have We Reached Peak Peak? The Rise (and Rise) of a Ubiquitous Phrase.' *The Guardian*. Published electronically 28 August 2014. www.theguardian.com/media/2014/aug/27/have-we-reached-peak-peak-rise-ubiquitous-phrase.

Colombia, Beatriz. 'Beyond Pavilions: Architecture as a Mahine to See.' In *The Pavilion: Pleasure and Polemics in Architecture*. Edited by Peter Cachola Schmal, pp. 64–78. Ostfildern: Hatje Cantz, 2009.

'Creative State.' Creative Victoria. http://creative.vic.gov.au/about/creative-state.

'Creative Victoria.' Creative Victoria. http://archive.creative.vic.gov.au/News/News/2016/New_Creative_Victoria_website_launched.

Crinson, Mark, and Jules Lubbock. *Architecture: Art or Profession? Three Hundred Years of Architectural Education in Britain*. Manchester: Manchester University Press, 1994.

Cunningham, Stuart. *Hidden Innovation: Policy, Industry and the Creative Sector*. Brisbane: University of Queensland Press, 2013.

Da Silva, José, Javier Pes, and Emily Sharpe. 'Visitor Figures 2016: Christo Helps 1.2 Million People to Walk on Water.' *The Art Newspaper*. Published electronically 28 March 2017. http://theartnewspaper.com/news/visitor-figures-2016:-christo-helps-1.2-million-people-to-walk-on-water.

Davidts, Wouter. *Triple Bond: Essays on Art, Architecture*

and Museums. Amsterdam: Valiz, 2017.

Department for Digital, Culture, Media & Sport. 'Creative Industries Mapping Documents 1998.' London: UK Government, DCMS, 1998. www.gov.uk/government/publications/creative-industries-mapping-documents-1998.

——. 'Official Statistics: DCMS Sectors Economic Estimates 2016.' UK Government, DCMS. 2016. www.gov.uk/government/statistics/dcms-sectors-economic-estimates-2016.

Feireiss, Kirstin, and Jean-Louis Cohen, eds. *The Art of Architecture Exhibitions*. Rotterdam: NAi Publishers, 2001.

Flew, Terry. *The Creative Industries: Culture and Policy*. Los Angeles, CA: SAGE, 2012.

Foster, Hal. *The Art-Architecture Complex*. London: Verso, 2011.

Fried, Michael. 'Art and Objecthood.' *Artforum* 5, no. 10 (Summer 1967), pp. 12–33.

——. *Art and Objecthood: Essays and Reviews*. Chicago: University of Chicago Press, 1998.

Garnham, Nicholas. 'From Cultural to Creative Industries: An Analysis of the Implications of the "Creative Industries" Approach to Arts and Media Policy Making in the United Kingdom.' *International Journal of Cultural Policy* 11, no. 1 (2005), pp. 15–29.

Google Inc. 'Google Trends.' https://trends.google.com.au/trends/.

Greenberg, Reesa. 'The Exhibited Redistributed: A Case for Reassessing Space.' In *Thinking About Exhibitions*. Edited by Bruce Ferguson, Reesa Greenberg, and Sandy Nairne. London: Routledge, 1996.

Hesmondhalgh, David. *The Cultural Industries*. 2nd ed.

London and Thousand Oaks, CA: Sage, 2007.

Hewison, Robert. *Cultural Capital: The Rise and Fall of Creative Britain*. London: Verso, 2014.

Holden, Susan. "'To Be with Architecture Is All We Ask'': A Critical Genealogy of the Serpentine Pavilions.' In *Quotation, Quotation: 34th Annual Conference of the Society of Architectural Historians, Australia and New Zealand*. Edited by Gevork Hartoonian and John Ting. Canberra: SAHANZ, 2017.

Jackson, Thomas Graham, and Richard Norman Shaw. *Architecture: Profession or an Art: Thirteen Short Essays on the Qualifications and Training of Architects*. London: John Murray, 1892.

Jacob, Mary Jane. 'Making History in Charleston.' In *Places with a Past: New Site-Specific Art at Charleston's Spoleto Festival*. Edited by Mary Jane Jacob and Christian Boltanski. New York: Rizzoli, 1991.

Jodidio, Philip. 'Interview with Julia Peyton-Jones and Hans Ulrich Obrist.' In *Serpentine Gallery Pavilions*. Edited by Philip Jodidio. Cologne: Taschen, 2011.

——. *The New Pavilions*. New York: Thames & Hudson, 2016.

Joselit, David. *After Art* (Point: Essays on Architecture). Princeton, NJ: Princeton University Press, 2013.

Kauffman, Jordan. 'Architecture in the Art Market: The Max Protetch Gallery.' *Journal of Architectural Education* 70, no. 2 (2016), pp. 257–268.

Krauss, Rosalind. 'Sculpture in the Expanded Field.' *October* 8 (1979), pp. 30–44.

Kristeller, Paul Oskar. 'The Modern System of the Arts.' In *Renaissance Thought and the Arts: Collected Essays*. Princeton, NJ: Princeton University Press, 1990.

Lamoureux, Johanne. 'The Museum Flat.' In *Thinking*

About Exhibitions. Edited by Bruce Ferguson, Reesa Greenberg, and Sandy Nairne. London: Routledge, 1996.

Lavin, Sylvia. 'Vanishing Point.' *Artforum International* 51, no. 2 (2012), pp. 212–219.

Leach, Andrew, and John Macarthur. *Architecture, Disciplinarity, and the Arts*. Ghent: A&S Books, 2009.

Liefooghe, Maarten. 'Critical Performance: Robbrecht en Daem's 1:1 Model of Mies's Krefeld Golf Club Project' (unpublished article manuscript, Ghent, 2016), based on the conference paper 'Replicas as Critical Architectural Performances: Mies 1:1 Golf Club Project' presented at the 68th Annual Conference of the Society of Architectural Historians, Chicago, April 15–19, 2015.

——, and Stefaan Vervoort. 'Een revelerend gesprek: de figuren van Thomas Schütte in Het Huis van Robbrecht & Daem.' *De Witte Raaf* 158 (July–August 2012).

Lippard, Lucy R. *Six Years: The Dematerialization of the Art Object from 1966 to 1972*. London: Studio Vista, 1973.

Log 20: Curating Architecture (Fall 2010).

Macarthur, John. 'Architecture, Heat and the Government of Culture.' In *Architecture, Institutions and Change: 32nd Annual Conference of the Society of Architectural Historians, Australia and New Zealand*. Edited by Paul Hogben and Judith O'Callaghan, pp. 366–377. Sydney: SAHANZ, 2015.

——. 'The Semblance of Use: Function and Aesthetics in Contemporary Art Pavilions and the Longer History of Ornamental Buildings.' In *Quotation, Quotation: 34th Annual Conference of the Society of Architectural Historians, Australia and New Zealand*. Edited by Gevork Hartoonian and John Ting. Canberra: SAHANZ, 2017.

——, and Andrew Leach. 'Architecture, Disciplinarity, and the Arts: Considering the Issues.' In *Architecture, Disciplinarity, and the Arts*. Edited by Andrew Leach and John Macarthur, pp. 7–16. Ghent: A&S/books, 2009.

Miller, Toby. 'From Creative to Cultural Industries: Not All Industries Are Cultural, and No Industries Are Creative.' *Cultural Studies* 23, no. 1 (2009), pp. 88–99.

The Modern House. www.themodernhouse.com.

The Museum of Modern Art. 'Young Architects Program (Yap).' http://momaps1.org/yap/.

OASE 88. *Exhibitions: Showing and Producing Architecture* (2012).

O'Connor, Justin. 'After the Creative Industries: Cultural Policy in Crisis.' *Law, Social Justice and Global Development Journal* 20 (2016).

——. 'After the Creative Industries: Cultural Policy in Crisis.' *Journal of Law, Social Justice & Global Development* 1 (2016), pp. 2–18.

Osborne, Peter. '"Whoever Speaks of Culture Speaks of Administration as Well": Disputing Pragmaticism in Cultural Studies.' *Cultural Studies* 20, no. 1 (2006), pp. 33–47.

Otero Verzier, Marina. 'Fair Trade: Architecture and Coffee at the Serpentine Gallery Pavilions.' *Avery Review* 9 (2015).

——. 'Tales from Beyond the Grave.' *Domus*. Published electronically 12 November 2012. www.domusweb.it/en/architecture/2012/11/12/tales-from-beyond-the-grave.html.

Papapetros, Spyros, and Julian Rose. *Retracing the Expanded Field: Encounters between Art and Architecture*. Cambridge, MA: MIT Press, 2014.

Phillips, Andrea. 'Devaluation.' *Parse* 2 (2017), pp. 107–119.

——. 'Pavilion Politics.' *Log* 20 (Fall 2010), pp. 104–115.

Piles, Roger de. *The Art of Painting, and the Lives of the Painters: Containing, a Compleat Treatise of Painting, Designing, and the Use of Prints: ... Done from the French of Monsieur De Piles. To Which Is Added, an Essay Towards an English-School ...* London: Printed for J. Nutt, 1706.

Rendell, Jane. *Art and Architecture: A Place Between.* London and New York: I.B. Tauris, 2007.

Robinson, Joel. 'Introducing Pavilions: Big Worlds under Little Tents.' *Open Arts Journal* 2 (Winter 2013), pp. 1–22.

——. 'Pavilions as Public Sculpture: Serpentine Pavilions.' *World Sculpture News* 21, no. 4 (Autumn 2015).

Rose, Julian, Hal Foster, Sylvia Lavin, Thomas Demand, Hilary Lloyd, Dorit Margreiter, Steven Holl, Philippe Rahm, and Hans Ulrich Obrist. 'Trading Spaces: A Roundtable on Art and Architecture.' *Artforum International* 51, no. 2 (2012), pp. 201–211.

Rykwert, Joseph. *The Judicious Eye: Architecture Against the Other Arts.* Chicago: University of Chicago, 2008.

Schaik, Leon van. 'On Pavilions.' *Architecture Australia* 105, no. 2 (2016), pp. 40–44.

——, and Fleur Watson. *Pavilions, Pop-Ups and Parasols: The Impact of Real and Virtual Meeting on Physical Space.* London: John Wiley & Sons, 2015.

Shiner, L.E. *The Invention of Art: A Cultural History.* Chicago: University of Chicago Press, 2001.

Szacka, Léa-Catherine. *Exhibiting Postmodernism: The 1980 Venice Architecture Biennale.* Venezia: Marsillo, 2016.

Tafuri, Manfredo. *Architecture and Utopia: Design and*

Capitalist Development. Translated by Barbara Luigia
La Penta. Cambridge, MA: MIT Press, 1976.

———. 'Toward a Critique of Architectural Ideology.' In
Architectural Theory since 1968. Edited by K. Michael
Hays, pp. 6–35. Cambridge, MA: MIT Press, 1998
(1969).

Ursprung, Philip. *Studio Olafur Eliasson: An Encyclopedia*.
Cologne: Taschen, 2008.

———. 'Narcissistic Studio: Olafur Eliasson.' In *The Fall of
the Studio: Artists at Work*. Edited by Wouter Davidts
and Kim Paice, pp. 163–184. Amsterdam: Valiz, 2009.

Varghese, Annalise. 'Following the Folly: Quoting,
Constructing and Historicising Paper Architecture.' In
*Quotation, Quotation: 34th Annual Conference of the
Society of Architectural Historians, Australia and New
Zealand*. Edited by Gevork Hartoonian and John Ting.
Canberra: SAHANZ, 2017.

Vidler, Anthony. *Architecture Between Spectacle and Use*.
Sterling and Francine Clark Art Institute: Williamstown,
MA; Yale University Press: New Haven, CT, 2008.

Wainwright, Oliver. 'Beach Café, Billionaire's Retreat,
Wedding Marquee: Second Lives of the Serpentine
Pavilion.' *The Guardian*. Published electronically
17 June 2015. www.theguardian.com/artanddesign/2015/
jun/16/serpentine-pavilion-second-lives-zaha-hadid-
toyo-ito-frank-gehry.

Willink, Rosemary. 'The Met Breuer: From Sculpture to Art
Museum and Back Again.' In *Quotation, Quotation:
34th Annual Conference of the Society of Architectural
Historians, Australia and New Zealand*. Edited by
Gevork Hartoonian and John Ting. Canberra:
SAHANZ, 2017.

Winston, Anna. 'Burnt, Recycled, Sold: The Fate of 2015's

Temporary Pavilions.' *Dezeen*. Published electronically 14 June 2016. www.dezeen.com/2016/06/14/2015-temporary-pavilions-fate-burnt-recycled-storage-sold-serpentine-gallery-milan-expo-moma-ps1/.

Index

John Macarthur is Professor of Architecture at the University of Queensland where he teaches history, theory and design. His research on the intellectual history of architecture has focused on the conceptual framework of the relation of architecture and the visual arts from the eighteenth century to the present. John is the author of *The Picturesque: Architecture, Disgust and Other Irregularities* (2009) and contributed to journals including *Transition, Assemblage, Architecture Research Quarterly, Oase* and the *Journal of Architecture.*
    ‹j.macarthur@uq.edu.au›

Susan Holden is a Lecturer in Architecture at the University of Queensland. Her research on the relationship between architecture and art has considered mid-twentieth-century practices concerned with a synthesis of the arts, civic form and monumentality in post-WWII campus architecture, and the design competition for the Centre Pompidou in Paris. Her research is published in international scholarly journals AA *Files* and *Fabrications* and she contributes to the professional journal *Architecture Australia.*
    ‹s.holden@uq.edu.au›

Ashley Paine is an architect and Senior Lecturer at the University of Queensland. His research is broadly concerned with the history, design and exhibition of building surfaces and ornament. His recent publications have examined topics as diverse as the history of striped façades, the reconstruction of architecture in museums, and the posthumously built works of Frank Lloyd Wright. Ashley has contributed to journals including, AA *Files*, *The Architectural Review*, and *Interstices*, and is co-founder of Brisbane-based practice PHAB Architects.

<a.paine@uq.edu.au>

Wouter Davidts teaches at the Department of Architecture & Urban Planning and the Department of Art History, Musicology and Theatre Studies of Ghent University (UGent). He has published widely on the museum, contemporary art and architecture and is the author of *Bouwen voor de kunst?* (2006) and *Triple Bond* (2017). He co-edited such volumes as *The Fall of the Studio* (2009) and *Luc Deleu – T.O.P. office: Orban Space* (2012). He was the curator of 'The Corner Show' (2015, Extra City Antwerp).

<wouter.davidts@ugent.be>

Research for this book has been supported by the University of Queensland and Ghent University. This book is one outcome of a larger research project 'Is Architecture Art?: A History of Categories, Concepts and Recent Practices' which is funded by the Australian Research Council (Discovery Project DP160101569) and has been conducted through the Architecture Theory Criticism and History Research Centre (ATCH) at the University of Queensland.

Authors: John Macarthur, Susan Holden,
        Ashley Paine, Wouter Davidts
Copy-editing: Leo Reijnen
Proofreading: Els Brinkman
Index: Elke Stevens
Design: Sam de Groot
Typefaces: Eldorado (William Addison Dwiggins, 1953),
        Computer Modern (Donald Knuth, 1984),
        SKI DATA (Tariq Heijboer, 2014)
Printing and binding: Bariet/Ten Brink, Meppel
Publisher: Astrid Vorstermans, Valiz, Amsterdam,
        ‹www.valiz.nl›

Distribution
USA: DAP, ‹www.artbook.com›
GB/IE: Anagram Books, ‹www.anagrambooks.com›
NL/BE/LU: Centraal Boekhuis, ‹www.cb.nl›
Europe/Asia: Idea Books, ‹www.ideabooks.nl›
Australia: Perimeter, ‹www.perimeterdistribution.com›
Individual orders: ‹www.valiz.nl›

ISBN 978-94-92095-50-3
Printed and bound in the EU, 2018

vis-à-vis

The vis-à-vis series provides a platform to stimulating and relevant subjects in recent and emerging visual arts, architecture and design. The authors relate to history and art history, to other authors, to recent topics and to the reader. Most are academic researchers. What binds them is a visual way of thinking, an undaunted treatment of the subject matter and a skilful, creative style of writing.

Series design by Sam de Groot, ‹www.samdegroot.nl›.

2015
Sophie Berrebi, *The Shape of Evidence: Contemporary Art and the Document*, ISBN 978-90-78088-98-1
Janneke Wesseling, *De volmaakte beschouwer: De ervaring van het kunst-werk en receptie-esthetica*, ISBN 978-94-92095-09-1 (e-book)

2016
Janneke Wesseling, *Of Sponge, Stone and the Intertwinement with the Here and Now: A Methodology of Artistic Research*, ISBN 78-94-92095-21-3

2017
Janneke Wesseling, *The Perfect Spectator: The Experience of the Art Work and Reception Aesthetics*, ISBN 978-90-80818-50-7
Wouter Davidts, *Triple Bond: Essays on Art, Architecture, and Museums*, ISBN 978-90-78088-49-3
Sandra Kisters, *The Lure of the Biographical: On the (Self-)Representation of Artists*, ISBN 978-94-92095-25-1
Christa-Maria Lerm Hayes (ed.), *Brian O'Doherty/Patrick Ireland: Word, Image and Institutional Critique*, ISBN 978-94-92095-24-4

2018
Jeroen Lutters, *The Trade of the Teacher: Visual Thinking with Mieke Bal*, ISBN 978-94-92095-56-5
Eva Wittocx, Ann Demeester, Melanie Bühler, *The Transhistorical Museum: Mapping the Field*, ISBN 978-94-92095-52-7
Ernst van Alphen, *Failed Images: Photography and its Counter-Practices*, ISBN 978-94-92095-45-9
Paul Kempers, *'Het gaat om heel eenvoudige dingen': Jean Leering en de kunst*, ISBN 978-94-92095-07-7